I0421910

THE BUSHCRAFT HANDBOOKS

TIME & DIRECTION

Illustrations by the Author

Richard H. Graves

The Bushcraft Handbooks
Time & Direction

This Edition Copyright © 2013 by Palmer River Publishing

Cover, Graphics and Layout by: Palmer River Publishing

ISBN-13: 978-1484822807
ISBN-10: 1484822803

About The Author

The author of "The Bushcraft Handbooks", Richard Graves, is a member of the Irish literary family of that name. A veteran of the Great War campaigns in the Dardenelles and the Western Front, the author became passionate about the bush at an early age. As an enthusiastic bushwalker, skier and pioneer of white-water canoeing, he foresaw how a knowledge of bushcraft could save lives in the Second World War. To achieve this end, he initiated and led the Australian Jungle Rescue Detachment, assigned to the Far East American Air Force. This detachment of 60 specially selected A.I.F. soldiers successfully effected more than 300 rescue missions, most of which were in enemy-held territory in New Guinea, without failure of a mission or loss of a man.

An essential preliminary for rescue was survival, and it was for this purpose that the notes for these books were written. These notes were later revised and prepared for a School in Bushcraft which has been operating for several years and continues to provide valuable instruction to Servicemen embarking overseas on active service in Korea and Malaya.

Bushcraft

As far as is known, "The Bushcraft Handbooks" are unique. There is nothing quite like them, nor is any collection of published bushcraft knowledge as comprehensive.

The term "Bushcraft" is used because "woodcraft" commonly means either knowledge of local fauna and flora or else is associated with the blood-sports of hunting and shooting. "The Bushcraft Handbooks" include a volume on traps and snares, but these are purposely-designed to be completely ineffective for native animals which are insect enters or grazers. These traps have been included because they would only be effective in catching predatory animals such as cats and dogs which have taken to the bush, and other "pest" creatures such as feral swine or goat.

"Bushcraft" describes the activity of how to make use of natural materials found locally in any area. It includes many of the skills used by primitive man, and to these are added "white man" skills necessary for survival, such as time and direction, and the provision of modern "white man" comforts as illustrated in the volume on bush campcraft.

The practice of bushcraft develops in an individual a remarkable ability to adapt quickly to a changing environment. Because this is so, the activity is a valuable counter to the over-specialisation so prevalent in today's society, and is particularly significant in youth training and character-moulding work.

INTRODUCTION to the BUSHCRAFT HANDBOOKS

THE PRACTICE OF BUSHCRAFT shows many unexpected results. The five senses are sharpened, and consequently the joy of being alive is greater.

The individual's ability to adapt and improvise is developed to a remarkable degree. This in turn leads to increased self-confidence.

Self-confidence, and the ability to adapt to a changing environment and to overcome difficulties, is followed by a rapid improvement in the individual's daily work. This in turn leads to advancement and promotion.

Bushcraft, by developing adaptability, provides a broadening influence, a necessary counter to offset the narrowing influence of modern specialisation.

For this work of bushcraft all that is needed is a sharp cutting implement: knife, axe or machete. The last is the most useful. For the work, dead materials are most suitable. The practice of bushcraft conserves, and does not destroy, wild life.

R.H.G.
April, 1952

CONTENTS

THE BUSHCRAFT HANDBOOKS

TIME & DIRECTION

The measurement of time, and the obtaining of accurate direction (from North) are not primitive skills. Of the two, direction is the more recent development, although to the Polynesians it is older than their awarness of time.

Obtaining time and direction without equipment is practical, and in general can be more accurate than the average person's watch or compass.

Both words, "time" and "direction", are inter-related because if one has accurate time, accurate direction is obtained in a matter of seconds, or if one has accurate direction (from north) then accurate time is immediately practical without a watch.

The methods given in this book have been proved in jungle and desert and are applicable anywhere on the earth's surface.

The subject of navigation has been surrounded by many technical words, necessary to the science, but in this work the author has attempted to simplify the whole subject, and endeavoured to avoid words which would have no meaning to the average reader.

Note to reader.—For Northern Hemisphere readers read North for South, South for North and reverse cardinal points.

Introduction

Although a compass is the accepted method of obtaining direction, it is not always reliable, nor is it of very great value in dense bush, or areas where deposits of iron affect its needle. A watch is the accepted means of measuring time, but the watch may be out of action, and therefore it is necessary to have other methods to obtain both time and direction.

Definitions

'Time' is our method of measuring the intervals between events. The most regular event in our daily lives is the movement of the sun, and therefore for everyday purposes time is measured by the sun's movement. The stars provide a more accurate method of measurement and are used by navigators and astronomers.

'Direction' is the line or course to be taken, and in this case can be considered as from North or one of the cardinal points of the compass.

Sun Movement

As you know, the sun crosses the imaginary North-South line (Meridian) every day when it reaches its highest point (Zenith) above the horizon.

Therefore when the sun is at its highest point in the sky it is North or South of you, depending upon your position on the earth's surface, and the sun's position relative to the earth's equator.

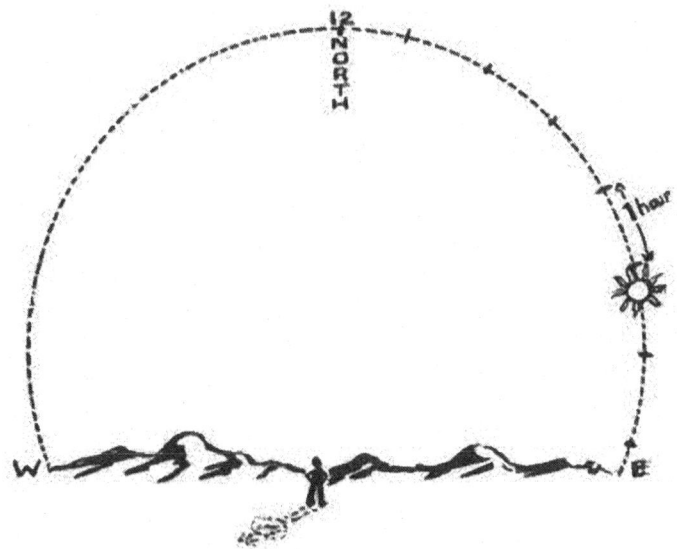

For all practical purposes there are twenty-four hours between each sun crossing of your North-South line, or Meridian. During the twenty-four hours the earth will have revolved apparently 360 degrees; therefore it will move 15 degrees for each hour, or one degree in four minutes. This is very convenient to know, because if you know the North or South accurately, you can easily measure off the number of degrees the sun is from the North-South line, and this will give you the number of hours and minutes before, or after noon. These measurements must be made along the curved path of the sun, and not on a horizontal or flat plane.

Time From the Sun With Compass

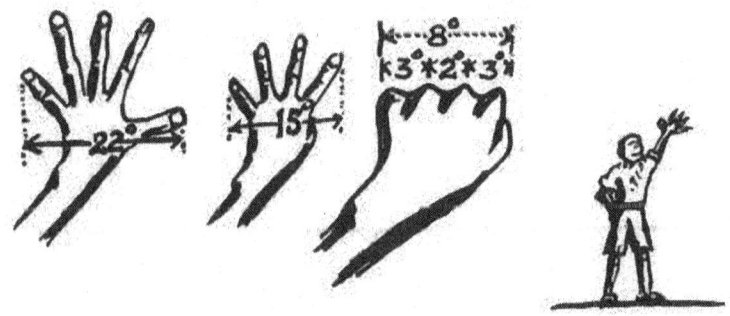

A means of measuring degrees—arms must be fully extended.

Hand at full arm's length, fingers widely spread 22 degrees

Thumb turned in . . . . 15 degrees
Closed fist . . . . 8 degrees
From second knuckle to edge of fist . . . . 3 degrees
Between two centre knuckles . . . . 2 degrees

These vary slightly like your personal dimensions and for accuracy should be accurately checked by each individual with a compass.

By this means, if you have a compass, time can be easily read from the sun's position. This should be possible to within four or five minutes. Decide from your compass your true North-south line and remember to make allowance for the magnetic variation from True North. Measure the number of degrees the sun is from this imaginary line, and multiply the number of degrees by four to obtain the number of minutes.

For example:

Here the sun is 34 degrees from the North-south line. It is morning, because the sun is on the eastern side of the North-south line, 34 x 4 = 136 minutes before noon; therefore it is sixteen minutes to ten in the morning local sun time.

This does not mean that it will be 16 minutes to ten by the local clock, because there are two corrections to be made before local standard (or clock) time can be determined. These two corrections are dealt with under the headings of EQUATION OF TIME, and LONGITUDE CORRECTIONS.

It is sufficient for the moment that you can measure

time accurately from the sun.

Accurate Direction From the Sun With a Watch

The method of obtaining direction from a watch by pointing the hour hand (or 'twelve o'clock' depending upon which hemisphere you live in) is not accurate, but only approximate.

The accurate method, knowing the time, is to calculate the number of degrees changed to minutes in time, before or after noon, and then to measure from the sun's position along the curved path of the sun through the sky. Even if you make no allowance for the two corrections (see section Equation of Time and Longitude Corrections of Time pages 326, 328), you will be accurate within five to eight degrees and if you make the two corrections for time you will be accurate to less than one degree.

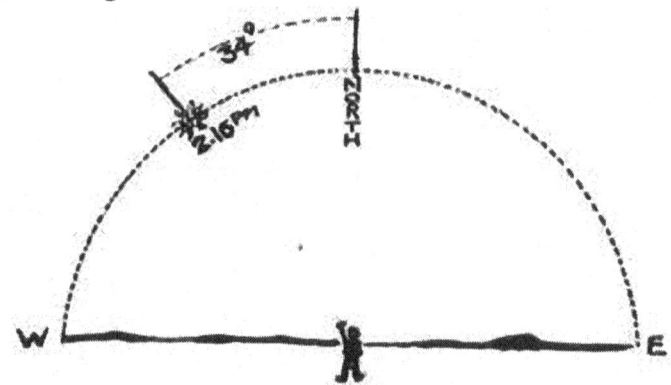

Example: It is 2.16 p.m. by your watch, therefore the sun is to the west of the North-south line. 2.16 p.m. means that the sun has travelled 136 minutes of time past the North-south line. It travels one degree along its curved path in the sky every four minutes of time, so that it is 34 degrees along its path past noon. Measure this back along the sun's path and you will have true North. (For Northern Hemisphere read South for North and reverse all other cardinal points.)

Cardinal Points and Bearings

Having found the true North, you can find any bearing from true North very easily and within five degrees of error. If the bearing you want is less than 180°, face East, and stretch out your left arm to true North. Raise your right arm along your side till there is a perfectly straight line along both arms. Your right arm is now pointing to South or 180 degrees True. Bring the two arms together evenly, and you are pointing to East or 90 degrees True, and you can then measure the number of degrees from these cardinal points to the bearing you require. By facing West, and pointing your right arm to the North and your left to South you can get bearings greater than 180 degrees.

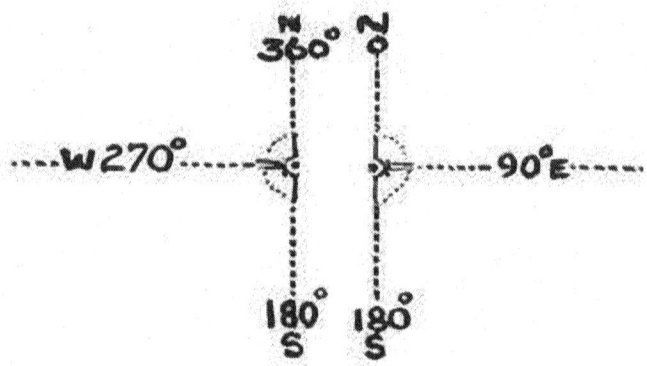

Finding North-South Line Without Compass or Watch

Knowing that the sun is at its highest point in the sky at midday, and that this point is on the North-south line means that by finding where this position will be, will give you true North.

You can do this by measuring the points of shadow made by the top of a fixed stake. These points of shadow may give you a curved line either concave or convex to the stake. Continue the curve made by the points of shadow, and then draw a circle on the ground round the base of the stake. Where the curved line cuts the circle will be accurate East and West, and a right angle from these two points will be an accurate North and South line.

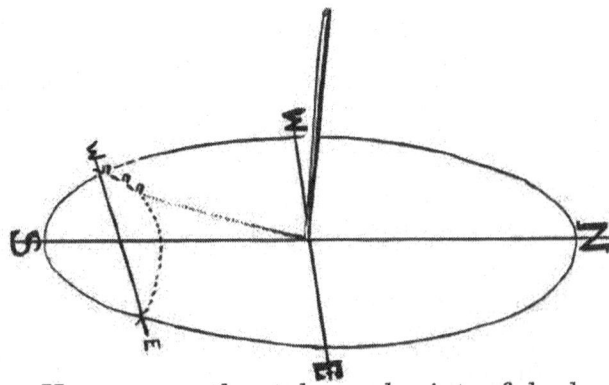

Here you see the stake, and points of shadow recorded over an hour in the morning. The dotted line is a continuation of the curve made by the points, and the intersection of this curved line with the circle gives you East and West. If North of the Equator the cardinal points will be reversed.

This Shadow-stick method is very accurate, if done over a period of an hour or two.

East-West Line - During Equinoctial Periods

You will find from the foregoing that it is actually easier to find the true East-west line than the North-south. The idea of always working from, or to, North is largely conventional. The top of every map is assumed, unless marked otherwise, to be North. All bearings are measured clockwise from true North, but in actual practice it is often easier to find one or other of the cardinal points, rather than concentrate on finding the North Point. An instance is the ease with which the East-West line can be discovered.

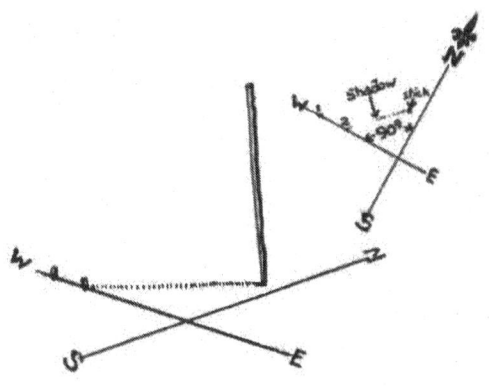

There are two days in the year when the points of shadow will form an accurate East-west line throughout the whole day. These two days are the 21st March, and the 21st September, the days when the sun is over the Equator. On these two days the sun is at right angles to the axis of the earth, and therefore directly over the Equator, and no matter where you are on the earth's surface the shadows will move true East and West on these two days. Because of this if you mark a point of shadow by putting a peg into the ground, and then, five minutes later, mark the new position of the same shadow you will have a perfect East-West line. For general purposes if less than 40° North or South latitude this method will serve you for about two or three weeks either side of the Equinoctial periods with reasonable accuracy, so that on any day between March 1st and April 14th or September 1st and October 14th you can assume that the shadow line is very nearly a true East-west line. At all other periods or when you want greater accuracy you will have to work out the curve and extend it to the edges of the circle as in the preceding section.

The points of shadow move accurately true East and West on March 21st and September 21st.

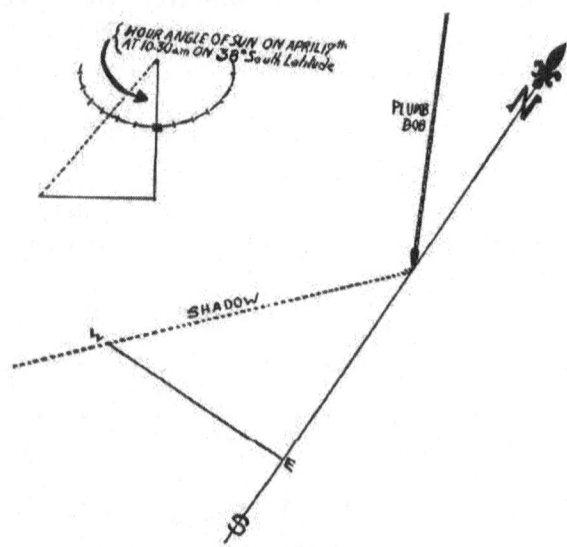

An extremely accurate method of finding true North is to work out the hour angle of the sun and transfer this hour angle to the shadow thrown onto the ground from the string of a plumb bob.

To find the hour angle, use the method given in the section on the sun compass and extend from the shadow of the stick, the hour angle correct for your Latitude and date.

The sun compass diagram does not require to be set correctly to work out the hour angle. Any direction will serve for the imaginary North-south line.

When the triangle has been worked out, a corresponding triangle is made on the correct side of the shadow from the cord of the plumb bob.

You should work out the hour angle on the sun compass on the ground about fifteen minutes ahead of the watch time, so that when you have worked on the diagram and made the necessary time and longitude corrections, you will be able to plot the hour angle at precisely the right moment on the shadow. This method, if done accurately and corrections of time for longitude and Equation worked out, should be correct to within less than a quarter of a degree, or one minute of time.

Finding Local Time Without Compass

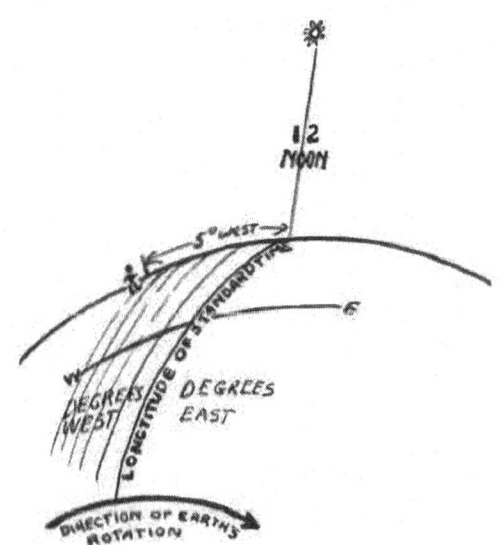

It is apparent that if you can find North-south by the method given from the shadow of the stick that you can then work out the number of degrees the sun is off the North-south line and thereby discover the correct local time, provided you know the longtitude of standard time, and the longtitude of your position.

The Sun's Path Through the Sky, and to Find the Sun's Height in the Sky for Any Period

To be able to accurately measure the sun's path along the sky you must know how high it is at its highest point (Zenith), and to find this out, you should be able to discover the sun's position North or South of the Equator for any day of the year.

This position of the sun is called 'Declination.' As you know, the sun is farthest North on June 21st, crosses the Equator September 21st, farthest South December 21st and recrosses the Equator on its way North on March 21st. This is caused by the inclined angle of the axis of the earth in relation to its path round the sun.

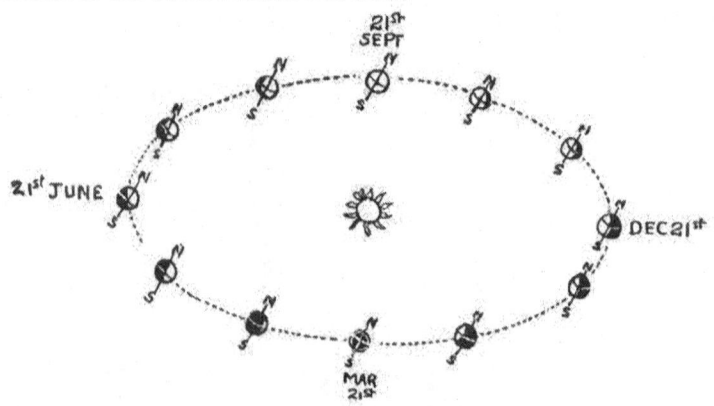

To Find the Sun's Position North or South of the Equator

The degree, or slope of the inclined path is approximately 23½ degrees, so that when the sun is farthest North it is overhead 23½ degrees North of the Equator, and when farthest South it is overhead 23½ degrees South of the Equator.

It is possible to work a circle of 'Declination' showing you the path of the earth round the sun, and the reason.

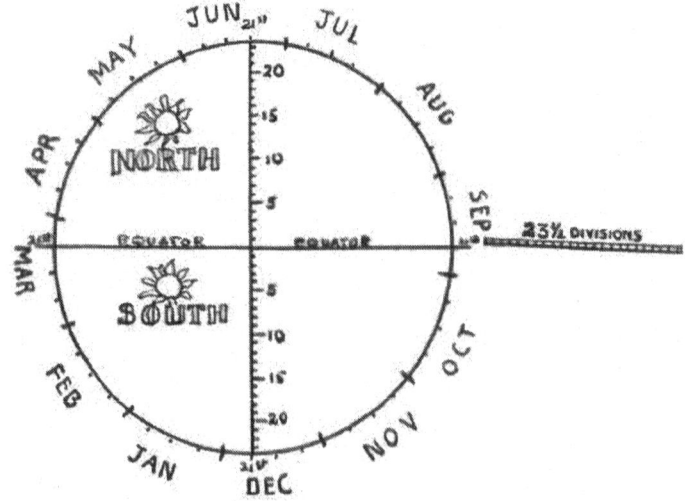

You can draw this diagram on the ground. Take a straight stick and cut 23½ divisions along its length. The size of the divisions must be absolutely equal.

If you use the width of your knife blade, or some equally simple measure, it will serve. With this stick as a radius, draw a circle on the ground, and divide the circle into four quarters with straight lines that cross the centre of the circle.

Now divide each quarter of the circumference of-the circle into three equal divisions. Mark these June, December, March and September as shown. Now divide each month into four smaller equal divisions. These represent the four weeks of the average month.

Draw a thick line from the start of the fourth division of June to the start of the fourth division of December, and from the start of the fourth Division of September to the start of fourth division of March.

These lines should intersect each other in the centre of the circle. The lines from June to December represent the North-south line, and the line from March to September the Equator.

For any day of the year find the approximate day on the outer circle and draw a line parallel to the Equator line to the North-south line, and then simply measure off with your stick the number of nicks from the Equator line, starting in the centre, to the date line. If the sun is on the June side of the Equator line it is North of the Equator: if on the December side it is South.

You should be accurate to within a quarter degree. This accuracy is needed for latitude work, but not necessary for the Sun Clock.

The Sun's Height Above the Horizon

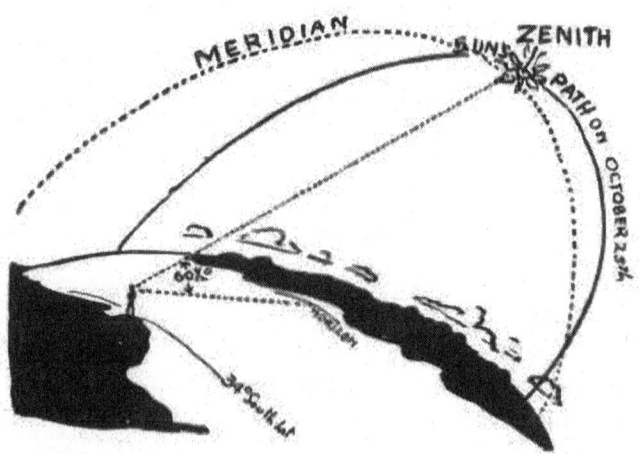

To the sun's declination you must make an allowance for your own latitude. For instance, if you are in latitude 42° North, and the date is April 21st, the sun will be 12° North, which means that at its zenith it will be 60° above the horizon. To work this out subtract your Latitude from 90°, and add the sun's declination. If the sun is on the other side of the Equator, subtract the declination.

Methods of Obtaining Elevation of Sun and Stars

Latitude: A degree of longitude on the Equator equals 60 nautical miles; therefore 1 minute equals 1 nautical mile.

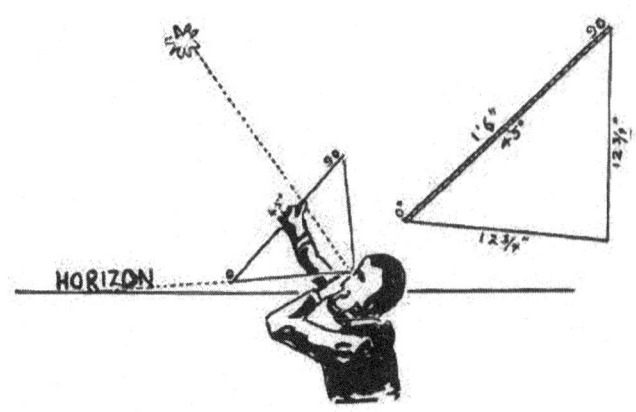

The elevation or height above the horizon of the sun or stars can be obtained by means of a plumb-bob quadrant-or, as Harold Gatty calls it in his 'Raft Book,' a Harp. The quadrant harp is made with two pieces of cord, and a straight piece of wood. The dimensions of both cord and wood MUST be accurate. The wood should be straight and smooth, and not less than eighteen inches long. Both ends should be flattened and a hole bored or burnt through the flattened ends. The holes should be exactly eighteen inches apart on their inside edges.

Through these two holes, two lengths of cord are passed, with a thumb knot to hold them fast. Two pieces of cord are tied together at almost exactly 12¾ inches (or if 36 board–string must be 25.45 inches) and where they are joined a third thinner length of cord for the plumb-bob is also tied so that it swings from the joining of the two cords of the harp. This plumb-bob cord should be about eighteen inches long. To the lower ends a weight such as a clasp knife or lead sinker, or a long thin stone is tied.

From the inside edge on one hole you mark off nine inches on an eighteen-inch harp or eighteen inches on a thirty-six-inch harp, and again a second mark an equal distance from the other end. The two parts should meet exactly in the centre of the stick. On one side of the stick along the nine-inch (or 18" side) side you mark the scale given in the margin. This scale is shown in short lengths for convenience, but for the marking on the stick you should read it as one scale. From 0 to 45° reads along one side on the stick and 45° to 90° along the other side, or alternatively you can mark the stick continuously from end to end. To use the 'Harp,' sight upwards along the cord at the 90n end till the cord is aligned with the sun or star. The plumb-bob should be swinging almost free along the stick, and when the cord is aligned the plumb-bob string will just brush against the number of degrees of elevation of the sun or star observed. You can get a reading accurate to ½ degree or less with this 'Harp.'

For finer readings–make the base stick 36", the cord 25.45" and make each degree on the scale twice as long.

(Readers interested are recommended to study 'The Raft Book' by Harold Gatty.)

Improvised Quadrant

Another method of obtaining elevation of a heavenly body is by means of an improvised quadrant, over a puddle of water, the surface of which serves as an accurate 'horizon.'

A useful measurement to remember is that a degree very nearly equals one inch on the circumference of a circle of a radius of fifty-seven inches.

A straight stick is marked off into 57 divisions of equal length. The actual length of each division is not important but the divisions must be as regular as possible. Another whippy length of cane or very pliable stick is marked off into divisions of the same length. These can be marked at five or ten division intervals to save work, but a smaller stick should be marked off into separate divisions for accurate reading between the five or ten division marks.

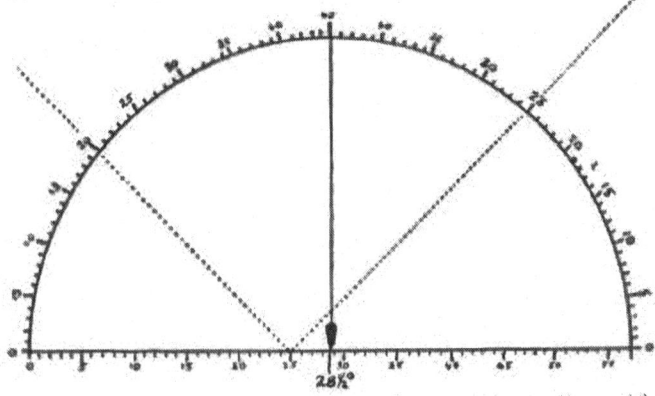

28½°

The straight stick is laid across the puddle, in line with the heavenly body to be measured, and the end of the ninety division stick is pushed into the ground so that the first mark is just level with the water surface. The stick or cane is bent right over till the other end comes to the other end of the fifty-seven division stick, and it too is pushed into the soft dirt beneath the water. The ninety division stick is then bent by hand until it assumes the shape of a semi-circle.

A degree very nearly represents one division on the circumference over a radius of fifty-seven divisions of the same length. The angle of incidence of a ray of light equals the angle of reflection, so these two facts enable you to use this bush-made 'quadrant,' and with no knowledge of spherical geometry you can measure the angle of elevation of sun or stars with reasonable accuracy.

Place your eye against one of the divisions of the semicircle on the side farthest from the object to be viewed and looked at the surface of the water for the reflection. Move the free hand or pointer stick along the far side of the curve till it cuts off the ray of light from the heavenly body.

Count the number of divisions from the water to where the finger on stick cuts off the ray of light and also the number of divisions from the water to the one against which the eye was placed.

The total of these two will give you the angle of elevation above the horizon of the object viewed.

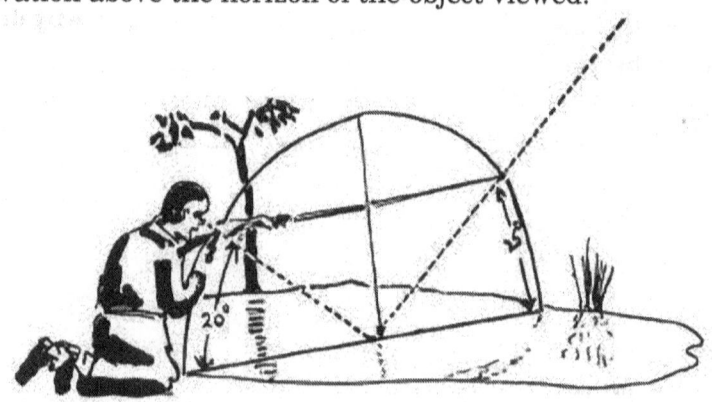

With care and accuracy in shaping your bow, and measuring the divisions you should be able to read to a quarter of a degree.

Equation of Time - and Corrections to Standard Time

Each day every longitude of the earth passes under the sun, but because of the slight variation in the earth's path, the exact moment when the sun passes over the meridian of longitude is not precisely at twelve o'clock every day. The difference may be as much as 16 minutes of time before twelve o'clock on your clock time and fourteen minutes after twelve o'clock.

This passage of the sun over the imaginary North-south line is called Meridian Transit' and as you will see it differs from clock time throughout the course of the year, except for four days (April 16th, June 15th, August 30th, and December 25th).

For convenience, the time of meridian transit is averaged out over the year, and the average is called 'mean' time.

The sun's passage of the meridian is called 'solar' (sun) time. The correction of time of the two is called 'Equation of Time.'

The following simple table on Meridian Transit can be shown in the form of the figure '8' for your easy memorising.

Time of Meridian Transit

January	1	12.03	May	1	11.57	Sept.	3	11.59
	6	12.06		6	11.57		8	11.58
	11	12.08		11	11.56		13	11.56
	16	12.10		16	11.56		18	11.54
	21	12.11		21	11.56		23	11.53
	26	12.13		26	11.57		28	11.51
	31	12.14	June	5	11.58	October	3	11.49
February	5	12.14		10	11.59		8	11.48
	10	12.14		15	12.00		13	11.46
	15	12.14		20	12.01		18	11.45
	20	12.14		25	12.02		23	11.44
	25	12.13		30	12.03		28	11.44
March	2	12.12	July	5	12.04	Nov.	2	11.44
	7	12.11		10	12.05		7	11.44
	12	12.10		15	12.06		12	11.44
	17	12.09		20	12.06		17	11.45
	22	12.07		25	12.06		22	11.46
	27	12.06		30	12.06		27	11.48
April	1	12.04	August	4	12.06	Dec.	2	11.49
	6	12.03		9	12.05		7	11.51
	11	12.01		14	12.05		12	11.54
	16	12.00		19	12.04		17	11.56
	21	11.59		24	12.02		22	11.58
	26	11.58		29	12.01		27	12.01
							31	12.03

A figure eight drawn to the proportions shown and with the four dates remembered when meridian transit coincides with mean time will give reasonably accurate corrections.

Note: The four dates when there is no correction are April 16th, June 15th, August 30th and December 25th, Xmas Day.

The top section of the figure 8 is about one-third the

size of the lower half. The horizontal line is divided into three five-minute sections to right and left, and the right side marked PLUS to mean that the sun is ahead of mean time. The left is marked MINUS, the sun is behind mean time.

The application of this 'Equation ot Time' correction will be required if you want to get accurate time from the sun, and also for correction to the sun compass-sun clock.

Longitude Corrections

The other correction which you will have to make to Solar time is a correction for longitude. Time for clocks on various parts of the earth's surface is called 'Standard Time,' and is based upon the longitude convenient for a large tract of country.

In England, time is based on Greenwich, hence the term 'Greenwich mean time.'

The areas of the earth and the meridian of longitude on which their standard time is based are as follows:

In other large land masses such as America, Africa, Russia and of course Australia, standard time may be defined as Eastern Standard Time, Central Standard Time, Western Standard Time, etc.

The areas of the earth and the meridian of longitude on which their standard time is based are as follows:

12h.	E	180	Siberia (E. Long. 157½ to 172½) Fiji Islands.
11h. 30m.	E	172½	New Zealand. Norfolk Island, Nauru Island.
11h.	E	165	New Caledonia, New Hebrides, Ocean Island, Solomon Islands, Siberia (E. Long. 142½ to 157½).
10h. 30m.	E	159	Lord Howe Island.
10h.	E	150	Tasmania, Victoria, N.S.W., Queensland, British New Guinea, Guam, Siberia (E. Long. 127½ to 142½).
9h. 30m.	E	142½	South Australia, Northern Territory,
9h.	E	135	Broken Hill, Area of N.S.W. Manchuria, Japan, Dutch New Guinea.
8h.	E	120	All coastal area of China, Philippine Islands, British North Borneo, Timor, Western Australia, Celebes.
7h. 30m.	E	112½	Sarawak, Java, Madura, Bali, Lombok, Dutch Borneo.
7h. 20m.	E	110	Federated Malay States, Straits Settlements.
7h.	E	105	French Indo-China, Thailand, Southern Sumatra.
5h. 30m.	E	82½	India (except Calcutta 5h. 53m. 20.8 S.), Ceylon.
4h.	E	60	Russia (Long. 40°E. to 52½°E.)
3h. 30m.	E	52½	Iran.
3h.	E	45	Iraq, Eritrea, French and Italian Somaliland, Madagascar, Russia (West of Long. 40°E.).
2h. 45m.	E	41½	Kenya, Palestine, Syria, Egypt, Union of South Africa.
1h.	E	15	Malta, Tunisia, Libya, Nigeria, Cameroons, French Equatorial Africa, Norway, Sweden, Germany, Italy.
0h.		0	Great Britain, Northern Ireland, Eire, France, Belgium, Spain.
+4h.	W	60	Eastern Part of Canada, U.S.A., South America.
+5h.	W	75	Parts of Canada and U.S.A., including Quebec and New York.
+6h.	W	90	Central States of Canada and U.S.A.,
+7h.	W	105	Central America.
+8h.	W	120	Mountain parts of Canada and U.S.A. West coast of Canada and U.S.A.

To make the necessary longitude corrections, you must know whether you are set East or West of the meridian on which standard time for the locality is based.

If you are East your sun will be ahead and you must deduct four minutes for each degree you are East of the meridian of standard time. If you are West your sun time will be later than the Standard Meridian and you must add four minutes for each degree you are West.

IMPORTANT

The corrections for the equation of time and for longitude are necessary to correct conversion of sun time to standard time for accurate direction, and also for accurate reading of directions and time from the sun compass. With these corrections you should be able to get local standard time to within two minutes, and a bearing accurate to within an error of one half degree, using no equipment whatsoever.

Daylight Savings Time

Sometimes a country will move its time back an hour from the standard time to get more daylight in summertime, and this change, generally called Daylight Saving Time, must also be remembered when making corrections to Solar time.

The four 'Times' you now know are:–

Solar Time or Sun Time: Local time of sun over the North-south line.

Mean Time: Average of Solar time over twelve months.

Standard Time: Application of Mean Time to a given area of the earth's surface.

Daylight or Summer Time: A local adjustment to standard time.

There is a fifth 'Time' you will have to learn, and this is 'Sidereal' or 'Star' time.

If anyone asked you how many times the earth revolved on its axis between midday of New Year's Day of one year, and midday of New Year's Day the next year you would probably say 365¼ times ... and you would be wrong.

The earth revolves on its axis 366¼ times.

The earth 'loses' one revolution in its path around the sun over the year and as a result the sun only crosses the meridians of the earth 365¼ times. This means that while the sun will only cross Greenwich 365¼ times a year, a star, which is far outside the solar system will pass 366¼ times every year.

For this reason Star or Sidereal Time is used by astronomers as being more accurate than Solar Time.

There is an extra day to be squeezed into a 'Star' year, a star day is shorter by 3 minutes 56.6 seconds than a sun day You can work it out for yourself. There are 1440 minutes in a twenty-four-hour day and these have to be shared by all days in a star year and that means that there are nearly four minutes less in a star day than in a sun day.

One degree equals four minutes of time, and so the stars advance roughly one degree farther ahead each night.

Sidereal or Star Time or the star charts commence for each year at the day of the Autumnal Equinox, September 21st, and for general purposes you can say the stars gain two hours every calendar month.

Accurate Time From the Stars

The star maps show the position of the brightest stars in their various constellations. The numbers 0 to 24 indicate the position of the stars at midnight at Greenwich on September 21st, when the star year commences.

0 means midnight at Greenwich, and every number means one hour difference from Greenwich.

Thus ALGOL in the constellation PERSEUS is on the radial line numbered 3, which means that it is three hours ahead of Greenwich. (Chart 2.)

This position of the stars IN TIME from Greenwich is called their RIGHT ASCENSION, and their position between the poles and the Equator either North or South is called their DECLINATION.

Declination is latitude, and Right Ascension is longitude The declination of the stars does not vary (as does the sun) throughout the year.

The Polynesians observed this, and regarded the stars

as 'fingers' pointing down to the earth and always passing over the same places and the earth revolved beneath them.

With the aid of the star map, it is easy to find and identify any star almost directly overhead. It may be slightly North or South but should not be East or West.

To find a point directly overhead, stand upright, with your head thrown well back. Rotate the body through a series of half circles and you will see the stars overhead appear to move in arcs.

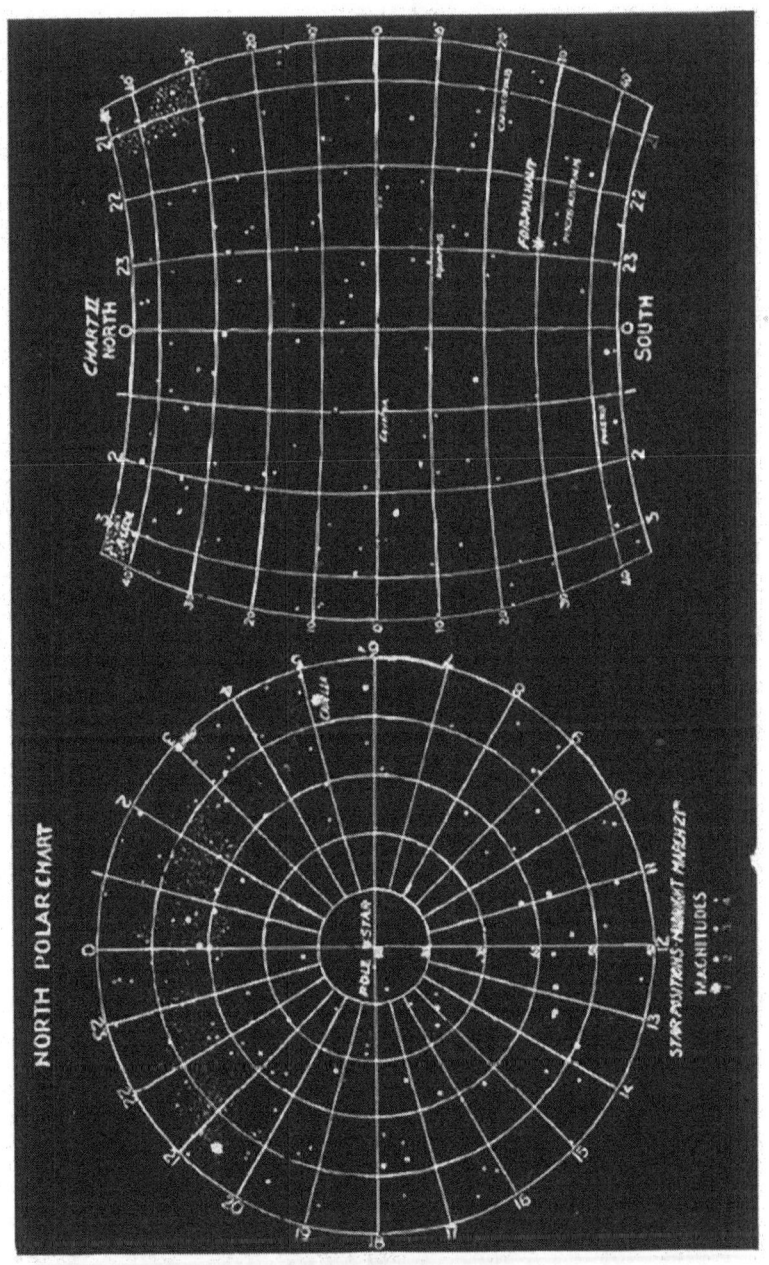

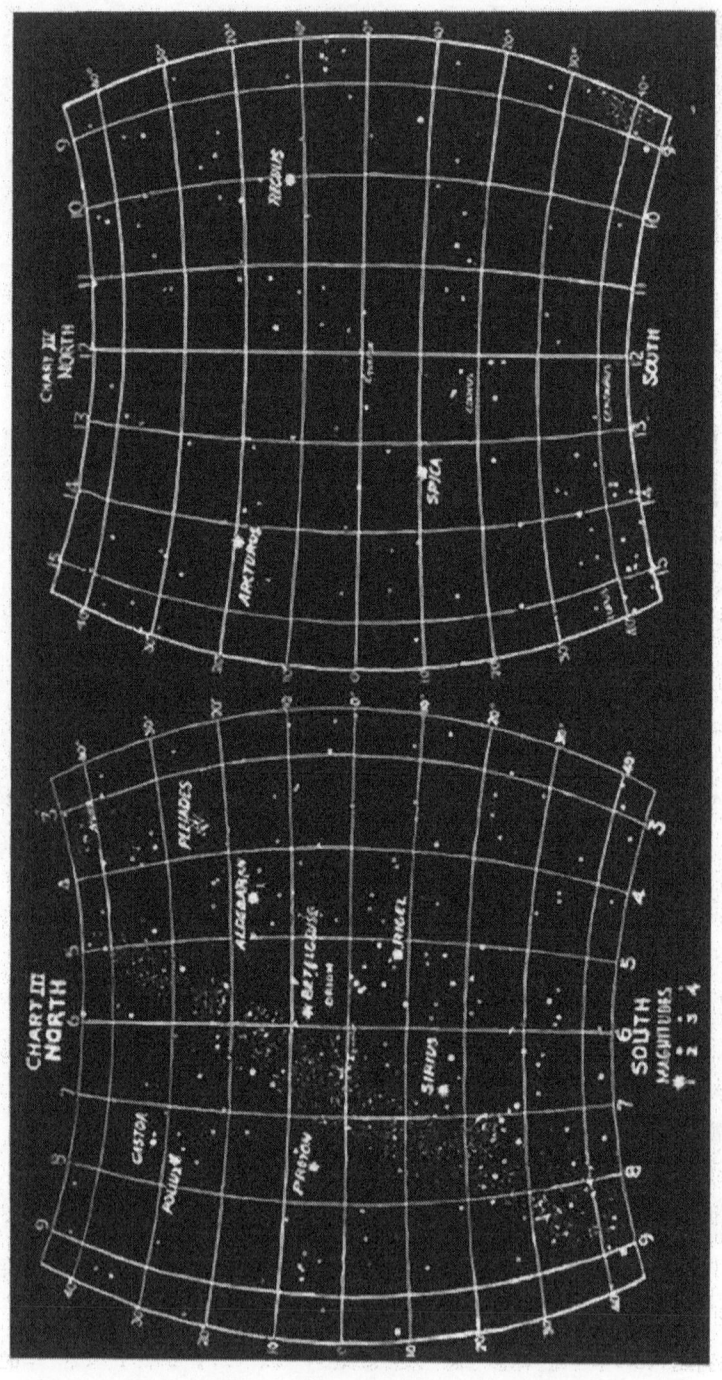

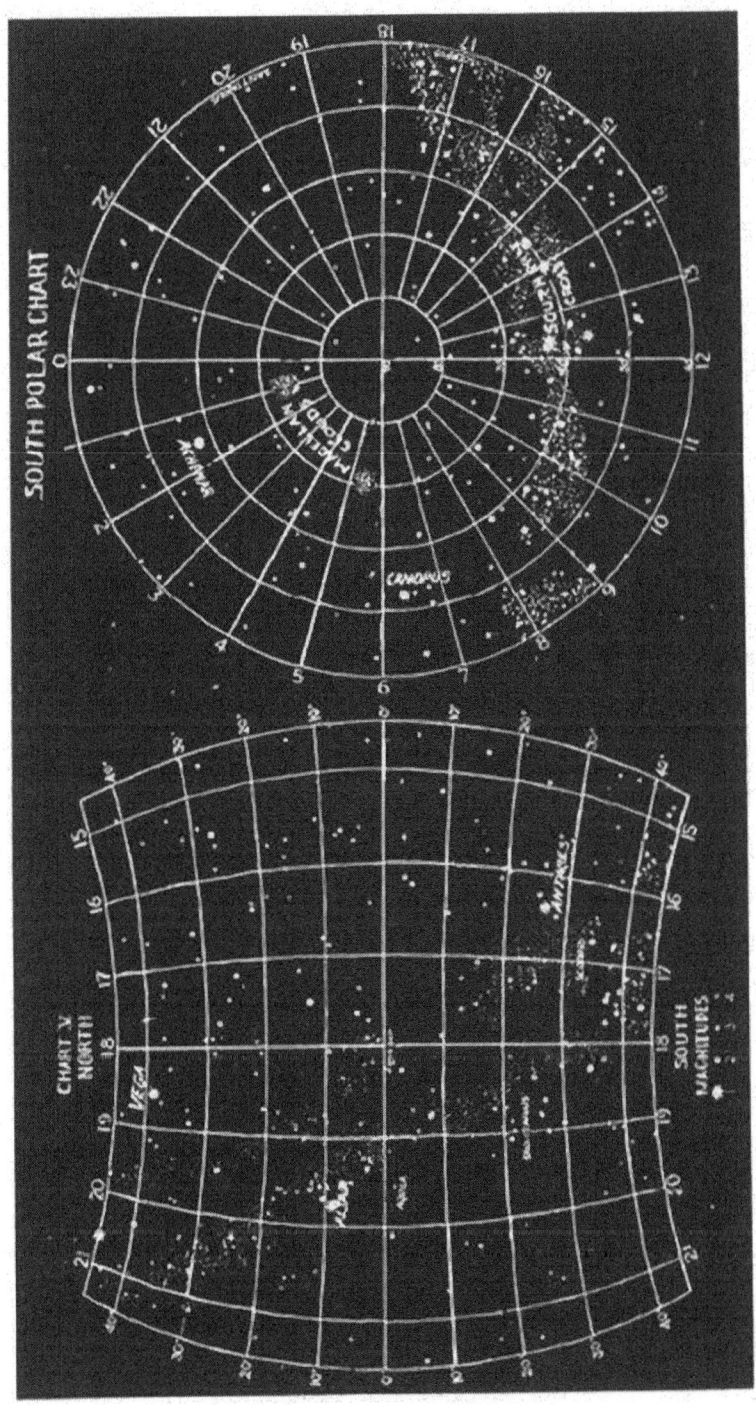

The centre of the circle which the arcs form will be the point in the sky directly over your head.

Having recognised the overhead star from your Star Map, work out its right ascension, and add two hours for every month, or half an hour a week and four minutes for every odd day till the next September 21st, and add this to the time of Right Ascension.

Example. The star Amares, the very bright star in the Scorpion, you read as 16 hours 25 minutes Right Ascension. The date if it is overhead is March 25th. From March 25th to September 21st there are five months, three weeks and four days, which equal a correction of 11 hours 46 minutes. This added to the right ascension of 16 hours 25 minutes gives a total of 28 hours 11 minutes. Because the total is greater than the twenty-four hours you must deduct the twenty-four hours and the result is 4 hours 11 minutes (a.m.) Greenwich. To this you must make correction for your longitude.

This method is applicable in all latitudes and gives reasonable accuracy.

Time From the Stars - Northern Hemisphere

In the Northern Hemisphere the stars appear to revolve anti-clockwise in the sky, and you must remember this when reading time from the stars at night. Imagine the Pole star (Polaris) is the centre of a twenty-four-hour clock dial, and the hours are numbered from Midnight 24 hours, anticlockwise with 6 hours at the left and horizontal with the Pole star, twelve o'clock immediately below the Pole star, and eighteen hours at the right, horizontal to the Pole star. The brightest stars, Alpha and Beta, in Ursa Major (opposite the handle of the Big Dipper) or plough are the hour hands.

It gives correct time only on one day in the year, March 7th, thereafter it gains 4 minutes a day, or two hours a month, so that if it reads fifteen hours on June 1st, it will be seven and a half hours fast and the correct time therefore will be 7 hours 30 minutes.

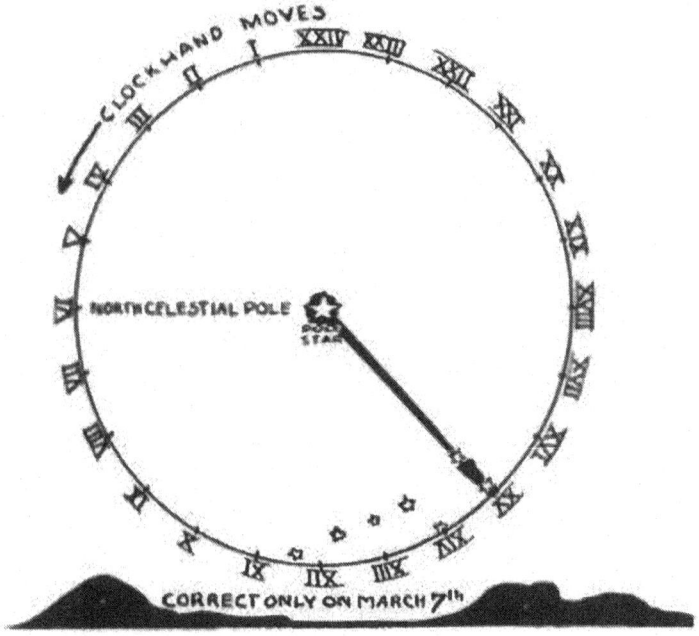

Time From the Stars - Southern Hemisphere

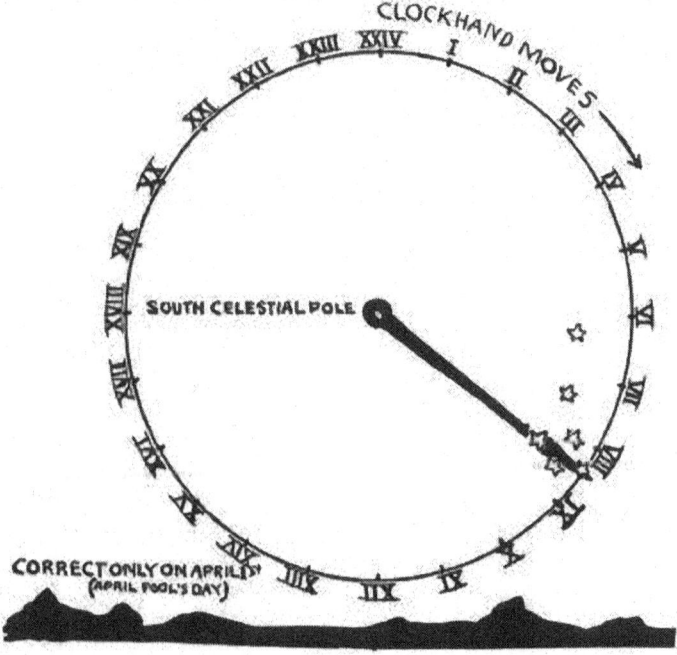

In the Southern Hemisphere the stars appear to revolve clockwise. The Southern Cross is the hour hand of a twenty-four-hour Sky Clock, and the centre of the dial is four and a half times the length of the Cross towards the foot along the longest axis of the Cross. This clock is correct on April 1st (April Fools' Day—just to fool you, but don't be fooled), and thereafter it gains at the rate of 4 minutes a day or two hours a month, so that if it reads 8.20 on September 1st it will be ten hours fast, and therefore the correct time will be 22 hours 20 minutes, or 20 minutes past ten at night.

Direction From the Stars

In the Northern Hemisphere, direction from the stars is easy. Polaris, the Pole Star, is very nearly directly over the North Pole, and therefore wherever you see it .in the sky is true North.

In the Southern Hemisphere there is no star over the South Pole and finding direction is a little more difficult.

One of the most popular methods is from the constellation CRUX, or the CROSS, better known as the Southern Cross. There are many stars which appear to make the shape of a cross in the sky, and therefore it is essential, if you live in the Southern Hemisphere, that you learn to identify the Southern Cross beyond any shadow of doubt.

Look along the Milky Way, which is unmistakable, and you will find a dark patch without a single star. This is commonly called the Coal Sack, and the Southern Cross lies right on the very edge of the Coal Sack.

To make identification more certain, the Southern Cross should show you five stars, the fifth less bright than the others, and nearly in line with the foot star, and one of the arms. Another certain identification is the two pointers, two stars of the first magnitude, lying always to the left-hand side of the Cross (when viewed as if the Cross was in a vertical position).

The longest axis of the Cross towards the foot points to the Celestial South Pole. That is, to a position over the earthly South Pole.

This, using the length of the Cross from head to foot, is almost exactly four and a half times the length of the Cross commencing from the foot.

You can measure this with fair accuracy by holding the hand at arm's length, and using the thumb and forefinger as a pair of calipers to measure the length of the Cross.

Another indicator of true South, suitable for moonless nights is the two Magellan Clouds, which form the base of an imaginary equal-sided triangle, the apex of which is over the South Pole. On bright nights, when these two clouds are not visible, the two very bright stars, Achenar and Canopus, also are the base of an equal-sided triangle with its apex over the South Pole.

The Sun Compass

A Sun Compass is far quicker to read and very much more convenient than having to refer to a magnetic compass. The directions for working out a Sun Compass are suitable for either working out on a card, on the ground, or, if you prefer it, for drawing on some unimportant area of your map.

On a map, a Sun Compass has marked military value.

A Sun Compass worked out on the ground in a camp becomes a Sun Clock, accurate to a minute if set down correctly.

First draw a circle (if on the map on a place where important information will not be obliterated) or if on the ground the area must be clean and level and open to sunshine throughout the day.

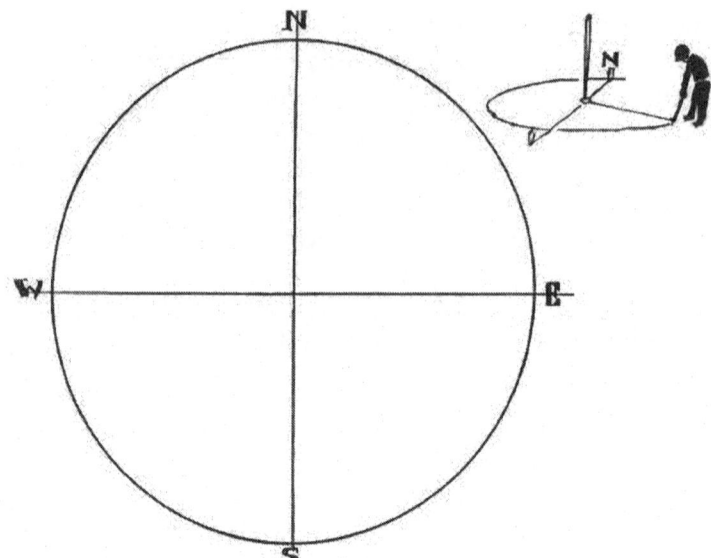

The first stage of working out a Sun Compass.

The size of the circle does not matter, six or seven inches on the map, two or three if for a card, three or four or even six feet if on the ground.

Work out carefully and accurately the true North line.

It is vitally important to have this most accurate.

If your Sun Compass or Sun Clock is wrong, it is because you have not put this North line in accurately.

If on a map this accurate North-south line will be either shown on the grid, or by the NORTH arrow head. Make sure that it is TRUE North, not magnetic.

When you have this line drawn from North to South, through the centre of the circle, draw another also through the centre from East to West, and divide the outer circumference of the circle into twenty-four equal divisions. Each of these divisions will be exactly fifteen degrees.

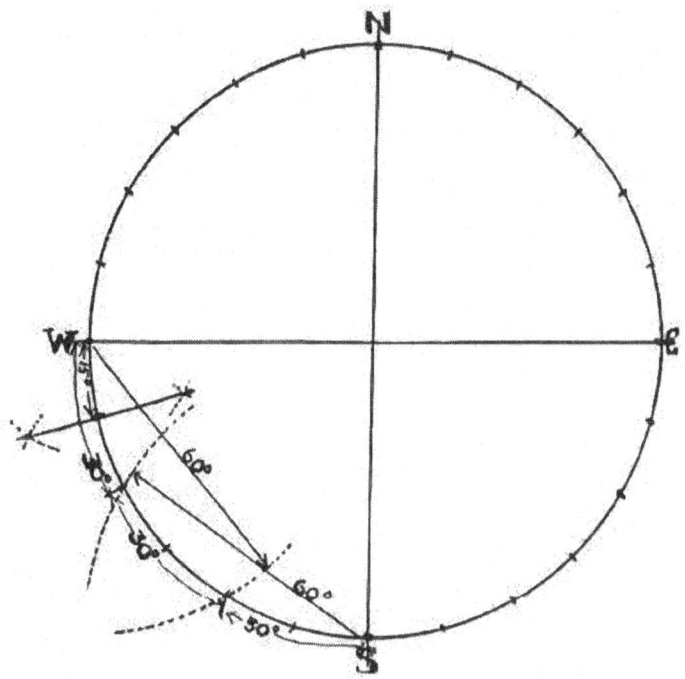

These fifteen-degree divisions can be either marked off, if on a card, with a protractor, or if on the ground by using the cord for the radius of the circle, which will divide the circle into sixty-degree divisions from the North-south points of intersection, and into thirty degree divisions from the East-west intersections.

These thirty-degree divisions are bisected, and as a result you have the necessary twenty-four divisions of fifteen degrees each.

Lightly connect these divisions with faint lines parallel to the North-south line.

Now consult your map if you do not know your approximate latitude (within an error of five degrees)' and starting on the East west line which is zero, come up for North, down for South, along the circle till you can roughly pinpoint your present latitude North or South of the Equator.

Mark off where this point comes to on the North-south line. You now have to draw an ellipse which will touch this point and also touch the East-west line where it intersects the circle. To do this put two pins (or pegs, if you are working on the ground) on the East-west line directly in line with the two latitude points on the circle. (By directly in line is meant parallel to the North-south line.) A thread or cord is tied to each of these pins or pegs, with its length embracing the pin or peg on the latitude on the North-south line.

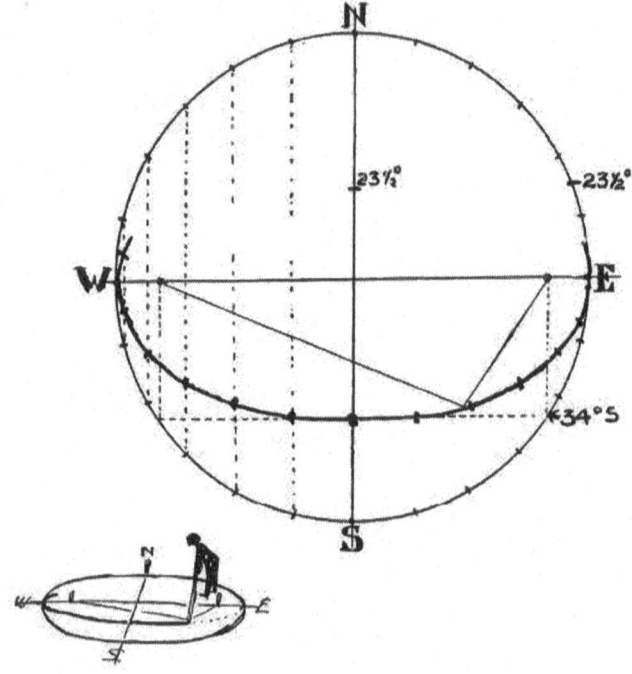

A pencil (or back of a knife if working on the ground) is put inside this loop, which is removed from the pin on the North-south line.

This will draw a perfect ellipse. On this ellipse mark in the hours, starting with the 12 on the North-south line, and reading to 6 p.m. of the East side, and from 6 a.m. on the West. (This is because the sun in the East throws the shadow to the West and vice versa.)

These hours are permanent and can be marked in ink, or with pegs or stakes if on the ground. (Roman figures are most suitable.)

The half and quarter hour intervals can be estimated by you with reasonable accuracy, and also marked in.

Now you must put in a declination circle to find out

where the shadow stick or gnomen should be placed for any day of the year.

Mark off the outer circle where the 23½ degree position is, and transfer to the North-south line. Using this as a radius, draw a circle from the centre of the big circle you drew first. Mark this off and set your shadow stick on the North-south line opposite the appropriate date. This shadow stick should be vertical, and should be set up with a plumb-bob.

The shadow will fall across the elliptical line, and where it falls is Solar Time. This must be correct for the Equation of Time (see method), and also corrected for longitude.

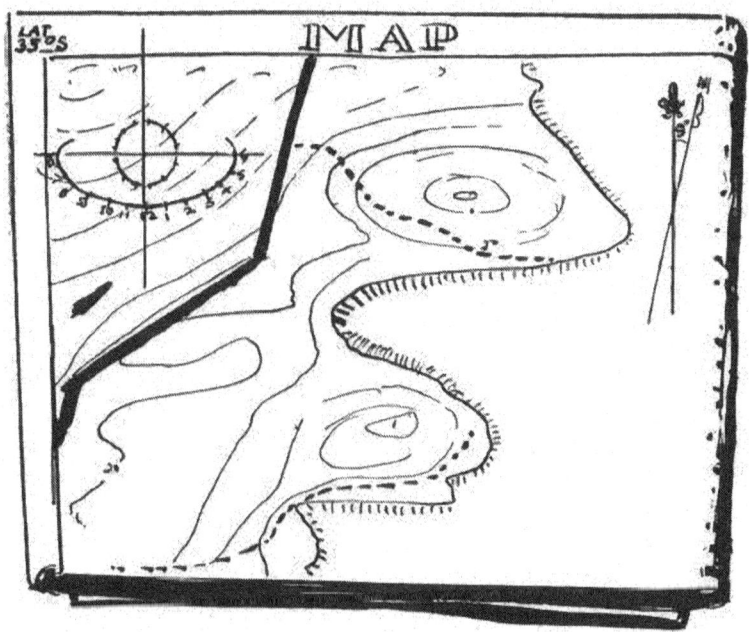

Note

A sun compass-sun clock drawn on an 'ordnance' (military) map can be used to obtain time accurately by orienting the map with the recognisable ground features, and then with the gnomen on the correct position, and the correction for time and the longitude corrections made, it should be possible to obtain accurate standard time within a minute or so.